ESSENTIAL OILS & ESSENCES

ESSENTIAL OILS & ESSENCES

A Practical Guide to Aromatherapy and Natural Health

SHIRLEY WHITTON

NEW BURLINGTON BOOKS

DEDICATIONS

To Rob
With my love

With thanks to my mentors:
Pierre Franchomme and Patricia Davis
and to my colleagues:
Dr Vivian Lunny, MD (MBBS), Consultant
Aromatherapist and John Sullivan, LSSM,
BAF, Senior Coach for their help and support
during the writing of this book.

A QUINTET BOOK

Published by New Burlington Books
6 Blundell Street
London N7 9BH

ISBN 1-85348-754-6

This book was designed and produced by
Quintet Publishing Limited
6 Blundell Street
London N7 9BH

Creative Director: Richard Dewing
Designer: Ian Hunt
Project Editor: Diana Steedman
Editor: Deborah Taylor
Illustrator: Katy Sleight

Typeset in Great Britain by
Central Southern Typesetters, Eastbourne
Manufactured by
Regent Publishing Services Ltd, Hong Kong
Printed by Leefung-Asco Printers Ltd, China

Contents

DISCLAIMER

Although scientific evidence is increasing, much of the knowledge contained in this book is based on traditional and empirical experience, and is presented for educational purposes only. The recipes are not intended as a substitute for professional medical care, and their application is undertaken at the reader's sole discretion and risk.

Introduction

What are Essential Oils?

Essential oils are tiny pockets of fragrance manufactured and stored in special sacs in the leaves, flowers, seeds, roots, and twigs of aromatic plants. Packed full of healing energy, they give the plant its perfume, help to attract insects for pollination, and allow the plant to protect itself from invading bacteria and fungi. This protection extends to us when we extract and use the oils because they can be antiseptic, bactericidal, viricidal and fungicidal, as well as anti-inflammatory, anti-spasmodic, digestive, sedative, stimulating – even aphrodisiac – depending on their individual plant chemistry.

Each oil is a unique and highly concentrated combination of natural chemicals. Plant acids, alcohols, aldehydes, esters, ketones, phenols, and terpenes account for their valuable therapeutic properties, and this fact has made oils the subject of close scientific scrutiny, especially during the last half of this century.

The Origins of Aromatherapy

Our remote ancestors probably understood the use of aromatics in healing far better than we do.

Many of the citrus, spice, and floral aromatics we now take for granted came to Europe from the Middle East at around the time of the Crusades. So, too, came knowledge and expertise, for it was in Persia that the art of distillation was finally perfected around the 10th or 11th centuries A.D. Physicians' prescriptions were taken to the *Al Attar* or dealer in perfume, and Attar (or Otto) of Roses, which was probably the first pure distilled essential oil, is still a vital and valuable part of any aromatherapist's kit.

Modern Aromatherapy

It was a French biochemist and perfumer, René Maurice Gattèfosse, who first used the word "Aromatherapie" in 1937. Most of his life was spent experimenting with essential oils, and his valuable work influenced people such as Dr. Jean Valnet (whose book, *The Practice of Aromatherapy*, is still a favorite) and Marguerite Maury, who combined essential oils with massage. Her passion for essential oils and the remarkable results achieved in her clinics in Paris, Switzerland, and London, are described in a fascinating book, *The Secret of Life and Youth*, first published in English in 1964.

How do Essential Oils Work?

Massage, baths, inhalations, and perfumes are the best ways to allow essential oils to enrich our lives. During an aromatherapy session, the benefits of smell and touch, combined with the therapist's skill, allow the oils to be absorbed into the body tissues. It is important to realize that oils can act on many levels and ideally should be blended together to suit the character of the individual with the problem, not just the problem itself. This book is an attempt to create remedies to suit everybody, but the reader is asked to bear in mind that the symptoms of an illness or a disorder are often just outward signs of a deeper, underlying cause, which must be understood and worked with if true health and wellbeing are to be achieved.

Extraction Methods

How do we get them?

Most oils are extracted by steam distillation, although some are obtained by solvent extraction and others, like the citrus oils, by expression.

Distillation

The most widely used and, as yet, the best way of obtaining the purest essential oils. However, the high temperatures involved make it less suitable for more exotic fragrances such as Rose, Neroli, or Jasmine.

The plant material is put into a still and then heated with water or steam, or both. The intense heat causes the tiny sacs containing the oils to burst, releasing their contents into the resulting vapor. This is then channelled into a condenser and cooled, causing it to become liquid once more. The liquid, which now consists of oil and water, is separated, leaving the pure essential oil, and a floral or herbal water.

Solvent Extraction

This is the most popular method of obtaining highly fragrant floral oils, although a slightly modified method can be applied to gums and resins. Here, the plant material is placed in a container with the solvent and heated so that the solvent can extract the oils. The resulting mixture is then filtered and becomes what is known as a "concrete." The concrete is then mixed with alcohol, chilled and filtered, and the alcohol then evaporates off, leaving behind the highly perfumed oil which is called an "absolute." More advanced methods of solvent extraction have reduced the need for alcohol.

Expression

This applies only to citrus oils. Here, the rinds, or zests, are simply squeezed by a machine (or sometimes by hand) to release their oils.

Enfleurage

A highly specialized and little used method of extraction reserved for high-quality flower oils. Freshly harvested petals are spread on fat on top of glass frames and replaced every 24 hours as the fat becomes saturated with essential oils. The resulting compound, now called a "pommade," is washed with alcohol which is then evaporated off, leaving the fragrant oil.

Masceration

A process in which flowers are steeped in hot fat which absorbs the oils. The plant material is then removed, leaving an "infused" oil.

Using Essential Oils at Home

Safety

Essential oils are highly concentrated substances and, as such, should be treated with respect. The following guidelines are important.

- **Make sure you use only pure, high-quality, unadulterated oils.**
- **Never use essential oils undiluted on the skin unless you are professionally advised to do so (e.g., lavender can be used in first aid).**
- **When blending essential oils with a carrier oil, always stick to a maximum two or three percent dilution for a body massage and a 1½ percent dilution for the face.**
- **For children under the age of seven, only lavender should be used.**
- **Always use the recommended skin test before you try any essential oil for the first time.**
- **Do not use essential oils every day, and do not use the same one consistently.**
- **Keep essential oils out of children's reach and away from your eyes.**
- **Never take the oils internally.**
- **Never use essential oils in place of prescribed medication.**

Massage

- **Do not massage over recent scar tissue, skin infections; if there are cardio-vascular problems; or cancer.**
- **Massage only lightly over varicose veins; the abdomen during pregnancy or the first three days of a period. Halve the recommended dilutions and avoid the following oils: clary sage, jasmine, juniper, marjoram, myrrh, peppermint, rose, rosemary.**
- **The following oils may irritate a sensitive skin: ginger, lemon, rosemary, pine, benzoin (if it is not pure).**
- **Do not sunbathe or use an ultra-violet lamp for at least 24 hours after using any of the citrus oils, especially bergamot.**

THE ABOVE SAFETY DATA APPLIES ONLY TO THE OILS REFERRED TO IN THIS BOOK.

For a full list of hazardous essential oils write to:
INTERNATIONAL FEDERATION OF AROMATHERAPISTS
STAMFORD HOUSE
2–4 CHISWICK HIGH ROAD
LONDON
W4 1TH
ENGLAND
or
consult a registered aromatherapist

STORAGE

If you follow these simple guidelines, your oils (except for the citrus) will have a shelf-life of approximately two years:

- Keep oils in amber glass bottles
- Store at room temperature and out of strong sunlight
- Buy in small amounts
- Keep oils tightly capped and do not open too frequently
- Check all citrus oils after three months and replace after no more than six.

MAKING A SKIN TEST

This is very important if you have a sensitive skin or are prone to allergic reactions.

Dilute one drop of oil into 1 teaspoon of carrier oil. Rub a little onto the inside of your elbow and leave for 24 hours. If there is any reaction, do not use that oil. The same procedure applies to carrier oils if you are not sure about them.

GIVING A BODY MASSAGE

Essential oils will not dissolve in water. They **will** dissolve in vegetable oil, and for some purposes in alcohol. for massage use a carrier oil such as sweet almond or macadamia nut, or occasionally in an infused oil, such as St. John's wort or calendula.

BODY

It is recommended that you use a maximum two or three percent dilution, that is two or three drops of essential oil to 100 drops of carrier oil. One measuring teaspoon equals 100 drops of oil.

FACE

Halve the dilution in a carrier oil. Do not stretch the skin and keep oil away from eyes.

Make sure the room is really warm and have plenty of towels handy. Sit the person the wrong way around on a chair, or have them lying on something soft on the floor, well away from drafts. Wear loose clothing.

Place the oil nearby in a saucer or bowl. Take enough oil to just cover the palms of your hands. Always put the oil on your hands first, never straight onto the body.

The three basic strokes in any massage are as follows:

EFFLEURAGE

Carried out with the palm of the hand, fingers together, usually on the back, legs, and chest. Firm, but gentle to soothe the mind and emotions. Deeper pressure is valuable in order to increase the circulation. All strong movements are directed toward the heart. Always work with the soft tissue only. Work very gently over the abdomen and never directly on the spine.

PETRISSAGE

Involves deeper work with the thumbs. Useful around shoulders, or on the calves, knees, or ankles.

KNEADING

Gentle rolling or squeezing of the tissue, rather like making bread. Best on fleshier parts of the body.

HANDS AND FEET

Use your thumbs here with just a little oil. A foot massage will relax and revive, and is very beneficial.

Baths

BATH

Run a bath at a comfortable temperature (not too hot). When ready, add a maximum of six drops just before you get in. Essential oils do not dissolve in water which increases the risk of irritation, so avoid the stronger oils such as black pepper, ginger, or peppermint.

CHILDREN'S BATHS

Use half the recommended amount and dilute in a carrier oil or milk first.

SITZ-BATHS

Half-fill an ordinary bath or use a large bowl, and add the recommended number of drops. Fold two small towels and place them so that you can comfortably squat with one under each buttock. Use another rolled towel to support your back, if necessary. Soak for five to ten minutes.

MOUTHWASH/GARGLE

Use only the suggested oils, two drops to a cupful of warm water. Do not swallow.

Compresses

Put the required number of drops into a cup or small bowl of water, and soak a large handkerchief or a washcloth in the solution. Squeeze out, apply to the affected area, and cover with plastic wrap.

Vaporization

STEAM INHALATION

Add a maximum of four drops of essential oil to a bowl of comfortably hot water. Cover your head with a towel and inhale for between one and five minutes. **Note: Those who suffer from asthma should not use this method.**

STEAM INHALATION FOR CHILDREN

This should not be done with children under seven. Reduce the recommended number of drops for children aged up to ten or eleven years.

FACIAL SAUNAS

A facial sauna is a large plastic funnel with a small plate inside, onto which water and a maximum of two drops of oil can be placed. When switched on, it gently fills with steam. Place it over your face for between one and five minutes. Splash face with cold water afterward. Good for oily skins. **Avoid if skin is sensitive.**

AEROSOL SPRAYS

A ceramic plant spray is the best type of aerosol spray. **Always use a spray with distilled water:** approximately 30–40 drops of oil to 250 ml (8 fl oz/1 cup) of water.

FRAGRANCE BURNERS

Fragrance burners usually consist of a small ceramic bowl with a candle underneath. Fill the bowl with water and add eight drops of essential oil. **Check that it does not burn dry and never leave it unattended.**

SCENT BALLS

A simple method of dropping essential oils onto balls of cottonwool. Useful for scenting corners or drawers.

Making Your Own Perfume

BLENDING

Putting a perfume together is rather like composing a piece of music. The perfume "notes" must harmonize with each other.

Essential oils are classified as Top, Middle and Base Notes, and a good perfume should have a balance of all three.

BASS NOTES are deep, lingering, and necessary to "fix" the blend. They often hang around long after the other notes have evaporated.
MIDDLE NOTES give heart to a perfume; they round it off and provide a balance between Bass and Top.
TOP NOTES are very light and uplifting. They will strike you first, but if they are not properly balanced with Middle and Bass, they will vanish in no time at all.

When you build your perfume, start with the Bass and gradually add the other notes little by little, shaking and testing as you go.

A SIMPLIFIED GUIDE TO PERFUME NOTES
TOP: Grapefruit, orange, lemon, peppermint, eucalyptus.
TOP TO MIDDLE: Bergamot, petitgrain, lavender, cardamom.
MIDDLE: Palmarosa, geranium, neroli, black pepper, clary sage, juniper, ginger, marjoram, pine, rosemary, rose absolute, ylang ylang.
MIDDLE TO BASS: Cypress, jasmine, rose otto, myrrh, sandalwood.
BASS: Frankincense, benzoin, patchouli, vetiver.

OIL BASED PERFUME

4 teaspoons jojoba or coconut oil
10–15 drops essential oils

Fill an amber glass bottle with the carrier oil and then add the essential oils carefully, drop by drop, shaking and testing as you go. Use roughly 10–15 drops of essential oil to 4–5 teaspoons of carrier oil. If kept tightly capped in a cool place for a week or so, the blend will settle and improve.

COLOGNES AND AROMATIC WATERS

½ cup distilled water
½ cup orangeflower water
½ cup rosewater
60–70 drops essential oils

Pour the water into an amber glass bottle and add the essential oils carefully, drop by drop as for the oil perfume. Keep in a cool, dark place for a week or two to ripen. Pour through a coffee filter paper and rebottle.

A NOURISHING FACE CREAM

¼ oz pure beeswax
1 teaspoon acacia honey
2 teaspoons sweet almond oil
2 teaspoons jojoba oil
1½ tablespoons rosewater or orangeflower water
1/16 oz soya lecithin
¼ teaspoon evening primrose oil or wheatgerm oil
3 drops essential oils

Put the beeswax, oils, and honey into the top of a double boiler and gently dissolve over a low heat. Warm the flower water to roughly the same temperature and combine the two. Beat until creamy. When almost cool, add essential oils. Pour into an airtight jar and refrigerate.

A GENTLE MOISTURIZER

1½ tablespoons jojoba oil
1½ tablespoons sweet almond oil
1½ tablespoons aloe vera
1½ tablespoons orangeflower water
½ oz cocoa butter
⅛ oz pure beeswax
3 drops essential oils

Put the oils, cocoa butter, and beeswax into the top of a double boiler and gently dissolve over a low heat. Heat the aloe vera and flower water to roughly the same temperature. Stir until cool. Add essential oils, then stir once more. Pour into an airtight jar and refrigerate.

The Essential Oils

The following is a list of the types of essential oils that are available:

Spicy

Black pepper, cardamom, coriander, ginger

Herbaceous

Chamomile, clary sage, marjoram, rosemary

Medicinal

Eucalyptus (blue gum and lemon-scented), myrtle, tea tree

Floral

Lavender, geranium, palmarosa, petitgrain

Exotic

Jasmine, neroli, rose, ylang ylang

Balsamic

Benzoin, frankincense, myrrh

Citrus

Bergamot, grapefruit, lemon, orange

Pine-like

Cypress, juniper, pine

Minty

Peppermint

Woody

Sandalwood

Earthy

Patchouli, vetiver

BLACK PEPPER

ENCOURAGING

The term "peppercorn rent" tells us that this old and revered stalwart of the spice trade often changed hands instead of money. A strengthener for the nerves, a tonic and antiseptic for the digestive system, black pepper gets things moving. It stimulates the local circulation, can ease stiffness and pain, and shift congestion around joints and muscles. ***It should not be applied where there is any inflammation.*** *Black pepper has been used to reduce fevers and to treat bronchial complaints, although it is not recommended as an inhalant. It can expel stomach gas and help in some cases of diarrhea and vomiting. Associated with courage, black pepper is an acknowledged aphrodisiac.*

PROPERTIES AND USES

EMOTIONAL: Fatigue, lethargy, lack of concentration, impotence.
RESPIRATORY: Colds, chills, fevers, airborne infections.
DIGESTIVE: Heartburn, diarrhea, constipation, nausea.
MUSCULAR: Rheumatism, poor muscle tone.
CIRCULATORY: Cardiac tonic, pre-sports warm up.
OTHER USES: Local massage, fragrance burner, aerosol spray.
PERFUMERY: Masculine fragrance, gives a lift to many blends.

WARNING: Too much black pepper may overstimulate or cause frequent urination. May irritate a sensitive skin.

LATIN NAME: *Piper nigrum*

TYPE OF PLANT: vine-like shrub

COUNTRY OF ORIGIN: Indonesia

PART OF PLANT USED: berries

METHOD OF EXTRACTION: steam distillation

MAJOR CONSTITUENTS: terpenes and oxygenated compounds

FRAGRANCE: warm, dry, spicy and masculine

CARDAMOM

FORTIFYING

A well-known culinary spice and a relative of ginger, this delightful remedy has been used for centuries as a tonic and aphrodisiac. It gently warms the stomach, easing heartburn, nausea and releasing gas. Cardamom is a good cardiac tonic and can improve the circulation, lift the spirits, and clear the brain – useful in states of confusion and debility. It clears mucus (although it is not recommended as an inhalant), and is sometimes used to treat urine retention. The seeds themselves can be added to potpourris or chewed to sweeten the breath.

PROPERTIES AND USES

EMOTIONAL: Exhaustion, fatigue, convalescence, lack of concentration, general debility, anorexia.
RESPIRATORY: Bronchitis, rhinitis, après-influenza.
DIGESTIVE: Gas, distension, heartburn, nausea, colic, bad breath, travel sickness.
MUSCULAR: Spasms and cramps, pre- and après-sport.
CIRCULATORY: Cardiac tonic.
OTHER USES: Massage, fragrance burner, personal perfume.
PERFUMERY: Adds a spicy mystery to many blends.

WARNING: Cardamom is not a recognized skin irritant, but be prudent since it is a spice oil.

LATIN NAME: *Eletteria cardamomum*

TYPE OF PLANT: reed-like herb

COUNTRY OF ORIGIN: Southern India

PART OF PLANT USED: seeds

METHOD OF EXTRACTION: steam distillation

MAJOR CONSTITUENTS: terpenes, alcohols, esters, oxides

FRAGRANCE: light, spicy-sweet, and uplifting

CORIANDER SEED

RESTORATIVE

This lovely spice is a storehouse of energy, and a tonic and stimulant for the nervous and digestive systems. The seeds themselves can be chewed to sweeten the breath, used as an aperitif, or a settler for the stomach. The oil is anti-infectious, mildly analgesic, gently warming, and revitalizing. Coriander is useful in cold conditions, to ease neuralgia and rheumatic pains, fatigue, general debility, and loss of appetite. Its stimulating fragrance can freshen the intellect.

PROPERTIES AND USES

EMOTIONAL: Tonic and pick-me-up, poor concentration.
DIGESTIVE: Cramps, distension, flatulence, diarrhea, nausea, loss of appetite.
MUSCULAR: Rheumatism, gout, pain and stiffness, minor cramps, neuralgia.
CIRCULATORY: General sluggishness, fevers.
OTHER USES: Massage, fragrance burner, aerosol.
PERFUMERY: Masculine scents.

WARNING: Use coriander sparingly. It can be soporific in high doses. Some sources suggest a slight risk of photosensitivity.

LATIN NAME: *Coriandrum sativum*

TYPE OF PLANT: aromatic herb

COUNTRY OF ORIGIN: Europe

PART OF PLANT USED: seeds

METHOD OF EXTRACTION: steam distillation

MAJOR CONSTITUENTS: alcohols (linalol), esters, ketones, and others depending on source

FRAGRANCE: smooth, fresh with a hint of aniseed

GINGER

NURTURING

A classic of Chinese herbalism and a Roman aphrodisiac, this familiar spice can be found in almost every cookbook and herbal. Helpful in cold, damp conditions, it warms the stomach and has the ability to regulate body fluids and raise body temperature. With a deeply penetrating nature that is more appropriate for long-standing ailments than acute ones, ginger is a good remedy for older people with wintry aches, pains, and congestion. Its fragrance alone can stimulate the digestive juices, producing a pleasurable sensation that is opening, stabilizing, and very reassuring.

PROPERTIES AND USES

EMOTIONAL: Fearfulness and withdrawal, fatigue, general debility.
RESPIRATORY: Chronic bronchitis and congestion, colds, influenza.
DIGESTIVE: Lack of appetite, nausea, diarrhea, flatulence.
MUSCULAR: Rheumatism, stiff joints, general aches and pains, lumbago.
CIRCULATORY: General sluggishness, low body temperature.
GENITO-URINARY: Kidney chills.
OTHER USES: Local massage, compress, fragrance burner, personal inhalant.

WARNING: Always dilute well; ginger can be a skin irritant.

LATIN NAME: *Zingiber officinale*

TYPE OF PLANT: reed-like herb

COUNTRY OF ORIGIN: Asia

PART OF PLANT USED: rhizomes

METHOD OF EXTRACTION: steam distillation

MAJOR CONSTITUENTS: terpenes (zinziberene), alcohols (zinziberol), aldehydes, and others

FRAGRANCE: full, sweet, and fiery

ROMAN CHAMOMILE

MOLLIFYING

*From the Greek "**kamai melon**" meaning **earth apple**, this well-loved English herb was often made into scented lawns. Roman chamomile gives us a gentle, yet versatile oil, which can soothe frayed nerves and is especially useful for children, hypersensitive individuals, or those prone to allergies.*

PROPERTIES AND USES

EMOTIONAL: Restlessness, irritability, anxiety, anger, resentment, insomnia, headaches, migraine, shock.
RESPIRATORY: Allergic reactions, spasmodic coughs and wheezes.
DIGESTIVE: Nervous dyspepsia, colic, stomach cramps.
MUSCULAR: Joint pain and inflammation, dull aches and pains, rheumatism, neuralgia, arthritis.
CIRCULATORY: Tonic and cleansing.
SKIN CARE: Sensitive, dry, inflamed, allergic, itchy, eczema, broken capillaries, earache.
GENITO-URINARY: Premenstrual syndrome, period pains, hot flushes, cramps, cystitis, and other urinary infections.
OTHER USES: Massage, compress, creams, facial sauna, bath, sitz-bath, fragrance burner, aerosol spray.

WARNING: Use sparingly and not in early pregnancy. There is a very slight risk of dermatitis in some people.

LATIN NAME: *Chamaemelum nobile*

TYPE OF PLANT: creeping herb

COUNTRY OF ORIGIN: Europe

PART OF PLANT USED: flowers

METHOD OF EXTRACTION: steam distillation

MAJOR CONSTITUENTS: mainly esters, with alcohols, ketones, and others

FRAGRANCE: fresh, green, sweet, and fruity

CLARY SAGE

INSPIRING

Often used to adulterate wines and make beers more heady, clary sage is a versatile remedy, ***but it should be used with care.***
It relaxes the metabolism, but can keep the brain alert and is useful in cases of fatigue and nervous exhaustion. Clary sage often brings restful sleep followed by a feeling of renewed vigor, but if misused, a night of unbridled restlessness can be the result.

PROPERTIES AND USES

EMOTIONAL: Nervous exhaustion, fear, paranoia, hysteria, lack of concentration, migraine.
RESPIRATORY: Spasmodic coughs and other respiratory conditions.
DIGESTIVE: General tonic, may help cholesterol and blood sugar levels.
MUSCULAR: Cramps and tension.
CIRCULATORY: Hypertension.
GENITO-URINARY: Uterine tonic, estrogen-like, postnatal depression, premenstrual syndrome, menopause, impotence, frigidity.
SKIN CARE: Inflammation, soothing, and astringent.
OTHER USES: Massage, compress, bath, fragrance burner.
PERFUMERY: Fine fragrances.

WARNING: Avoid during pregnancy, mastitis, and the second half of the menstrual cycle. Do not drink or drive immediately after use.

LATIN NAME: *Salvia sclarea*

TYPE OF PLANT: fragrant herb

COUNTRY OF ORIGIN: Mediterranean

PART OF PLANT USED: leaves and flowering heads

METHOD OF EXTRACTION: steam distillation

MAJOR CONSTITUENTS: a complexity of terpenes, alcohols (sclariol), esters, oxides, coumarins, and others

FRAGRANCE: nutty, smoky, with sweet, herbaceous undertones

SWEET MARJORAM

PENETRATING

Cultivated in monastery gardens in the Middle Ages for "cold diseases of the head, stomach, sinews and other parts," this welcoming remedy relaxes tissues and provides local warmth when treating muscular and rheumatic pains, strains, and stiffness, especially in cold weather. Sweet marjoram is very good for tension headaches and wonderful in a warm bath after a long, strenuous day; blend with lavender to give a good night's sleep.

PROPERTIES AND USES

EMOTIONAL: Mildly tranquilizing, insomnia, grief, worry, hopelessness, headache, migraine.
RESPIRATORY: Bronchitis, sinusitis, colds, influenza, breathlessness, irritating coughs.
DIGESTIVE: Diarrhea, constipation, colic.
MUSCULAR: Cramps, strains, stiffness, rheumatism, arthritis, neuralgia.
CIRCULATORY: Dilates tiny capillaries, aids detoxification, hypertension, palpitations.
GENITO-URINARY: Premenstrual syndrome, period pains.
OTHER USES: Massage, compress, bath, inhalant, fragrance burner, aerosol spray.

WARNING: Use in moderation. Avoid during pregnancy. Do not use on small children or babies.

LATIN NAME: *Origanum majorana*

TYPE OF PLANT: fragrant herb

COUNTRY OF ORIGIN: Mediterranean

PART OF PLANT USED: whole plant

METHOD OF EXTRACTION: distillation

MAJOR CONSTITUENTS: terpenes, alcohols, esters, oxides

FRAGRANCE: warm, herbaceous, camphoraceous

ROSEMARY

STIMULATING

"Here's Rosemary, that's for Remembrance," said Shakespeare and it certainly can sharpen the memory. Rosemary benefits the circulation and flow of oxygen in the body, helping to shift fluid and expel toxins, and it has a reputation as a liver tonic with the ability to help with the digestion of fats. It is an expectorant with a clean, fresh smell that has a purifying effect and is profoundly uplifting in times of colds, influenza, and general debility.

PROPERTIES AND USES

EMOTIONAL: Depression, confusion, lethargy, fatigue, general debility.
RESPIRATORY: Bronchitis, sinusitis, and other respiratory conditions (**inhale only in small quantities**), airborne germs.
DIGESTIVE: Liver tonic, gastroenteritis, hangover.
MUSCULAR: Rheumatic aches, pains and stiffness, pre- and après-sport.
CIRCULATORY: Stimulating and cleansing, gout, fluid retention.
SKINCARE: Hair and scalp tonic, cellulite.
OTHER USES: Massage, inhalant, fragrance burner, aerosol, personal perfume, scent balls.
PERFUMERY: Colognes and toilet waters.

WARNING: Avoid during pregnancy. Do not use on epileptics, young children, babies, or people with high blood pressure.
May irritate a sensitive skin.

LATIN NAME: *Rosemarinus officinalis*

TYPE OF PLANT: evergreen shrub

COUNTRY OF ORIGIN: Mediterranean

PART OF PLANT USED: leaves

METHOD OF EXTRACTION: steam distillation

MAJOR CONSTITUENTS: terpenes, alcohols, esters, ketones (borneone camphor), oxides (cineol), (depending on type)

FRAGRANCE: fresh, piercing, herbaceous, and slightly woody

EUCALYPTUS
(BLUE GUM)

MEDICINAL

There are hundreds of species of eucalyptus, but blue gum's reputation is almost universal. A favorite inhalant, aerial antiseptic, and chest rub, in winter it brings the warmth of its native sunshine; and in hot, humid weather, it cools and disinfects the atmosphere. As a mild rubefacient, it helps to ease muscular and rheumatic pains, and its antifungal quality makes it useful in skin care.

PROPERTIES AND USES

EMOTIONAL: Refreshing and stimulating.
RESPIRATORY: Colds, influenza, bronchitis, fevers, airborne infections.
DIGESTIVE: Diarrhea, gastroenteritis.
MUSCULAR: Rheumatism, joint pain and stiffness, pre- and après-sport.
CIRCULATORY: Tonic.
GENITO-URINARY: Urinary tract infections, kidney chills.
SKIN CARE: Oily, fungal infections, cold sores.
OTHER USES: Massage, compress, bath, sitz-bath, inhalant, fragrance burner, aerosol spray.

WARNING: Do not use on small children, babies or in conjunction with a homeopathic remedy.

LATIN NAME: *Eucalyptus globulus*

TYPE OF PLANT: tall, evergreen tree

COUNTRY OF ORIGIN: Australia

PART OF PLANT USED: leaves

METHOD OF EXTRACTION: steam distillation

MAJOR CONSTITUENTS: alcohols, terpenes, ketones, oxides (Eucalyptol)

FRAGRANCE: sharp, camphoraceous, with an underlying sweetness

EUCALYPTUS
LEMON SCENTED

CALMING

Gentler than its cousin Eucalyptus globulus, *this soothing, relaxing oil is particularly useful when summer colds or infections are bringing you down. It makes a lovely room spray in hot, humid conditions when fungal infections are likely and is also welcome in winter sickrooms, especially for children, when its gentleness makes it a good alternative to stronger oils.*

PROPERTIES AND USES

EMOTIONAL: Sedative, calming, relaxing.
RESPIRATORY: Mild respiratory conditions, colds, influenza, airborne infections.
MUSCULAR: Rheumatism, arthritis.
CIRCULATORY: Cleansing.
GENITO-URINARY: Cystitis, thrush.
SKIN CARE: Fungal infections, herpes, dandruff, deodorant, cellulite.
OTHER USES: Massage, compress, bath, sitz-bath, fragrance burner, inhalant, aerosol spray.
PERFUMERY: Colognes, aftershaves, air fresheners.

WARNING: Lemon-scented eucalyptus can cause sensitization in certain people.

LATIN NAME: *Eucalyptus citriodora*

TYPE OF PLANT: tall, evergreen tree

COUNTRY OF ORIGIN: Australia

PART OF PLANT USED: leaves and twigs

METHOD OF EXTRACTION: steam distillation

MAJOR CONSTITUENTS: alcohols, esters, aldehydes (mainly citronellal)

FRAGRANCE: balsamic, yet sweetly citrus

HONEY MYRTLE

COMFORTING

Associated with Venus in Greek mythology, this kind and gentle remedy is especially good for children's coughs and colds, as an alternative to more powerful oils such as eucalyptus. Mildly antiseptic, relaxing and decongesting, as a chest rub it will ease breathing, and help to promote sleep. Antiseptic for the skin, and a mild tonic and deodorant, honey myrtle makes a good inhalant for many respiratory conditions, particularly those connected with pollution or smoke.

PROPERTIES AND USES

EMOTIONAL: Depression, negativity, seasonal affective disorder, people with learning difficulties.
RESPIRATORY: Bronchitis, catarrh, sinusitis, colds, influenza, airborne infections.
GENITO-URINARY: Mild urinary infections, prostatitis.
SKIN CARE: Acne, oily, congested, bites and stings.
OTHER USES: Massage, bath, inhalant, fragrance burner, aerosol spray.

LATIN NAME: *Myrtus communis*

TYPE OF PLANT: small tree

COUNTRY OF ORIGIN: North Africa

PART OF PLANT USED: leaves and twigs

METHOD OF EXTRACTION: steam distillation

MAJOR CONSTITUENTS: alcohols, esters, oxides (cineol) and others

FRAGRANCE: warm, balsamic and slightly spicy

TEA TREE

ANTISEPTIC

Primarily a first-aid oil, tea tree is a gentle, yet powerful disinfectant and antifungal agent capable of dealing with a variety of infections. Known to the Aborigines for centuries, it is now a standard ingredient in creams, soaps, lotions, and shampoos and it is used to treat wounds and many skin conditions. Tea tree may help to bring down a feverish cold and can ease many childhood illnesses. A good immuno-stimulant and cardiac tonic and helpful in some cases of shock.

PROPERTIES AND USES

EMOTIONAL: Nervous debility, shock.
RESPIRATORY: Colds, influenza, bronchitis, catarrh, sinusitis, sore throat, airborne infections.
DIGESTIVE: Gastroenteritis.
CIRCULATORY: Cardiac tonic, immuno-stimulant.
GENITO-URINARY: Vaginal thrush and urinary tract infections.
SKIN CARE: Athlete's foot, oral thrush, acne, herpes, verrucae, cuts and abrasions, chickenpox, dandruff, mouth and skin wash.
OTHER USES: Massage, compress, creams, bath, sitz-bath, inhalant, aerosol spray.

WARNING: Tea tree may occasionally irritate the skin and can be blended with lavender to soften its effect.

LATIN NAME: *Melaleuca alternifolia*

TYPE OF PLANT: small, shrubby tree

COUNTRY OF ORIGIN: Australia

PART OF PLANT USED: leaves and twigs

METHOD OF EXTRACTION: steam distillation

MAJOR CONSTITUENTS: terpenes, alcohols, oxides

FRAGRANCE: medicinal and camphoraceous

LAVENDER

HARMONIZING

From the Latin "lavare" meaning to wash, this familiar fragrance has a clean and respectable image. Gentle and versatile, and a must for the first-aid kit, it is both tonic and sedative, and applied undiluted to the temples it can often cure a headache and bring restful sleep. A digestive aid and helper for many childhood ailments, easing cramps, colics, nausea, premenstrual syndrome, and shock, lavender is also a good skin antiseptic, especially for cuts and burns. It encourages the growth of new skin cells and makes a good local wash and toilet water.

PROPERTIES AND USES

EMOTIONAL: Insomnia, anxiety, depression, headaches, migraine, shock, fainting, irritability, fatigue.
RESPIRATORY: Coughs, colds, sore throat, fever, bronchitis, sinusitis, aerial antiseptic.
DIGESTIVE: Stomach cramps, nausea.
MUSCULAR: Aches, pains, stiffness, pre- and après-sport.
CIRCULATORY: Rapid heartbeat, general sluggishness, hypertension.
GENITO-URINARY: Premenstrual syndrome, painful periods, vaginal and urinary tract infections.
SKIN CARE: All types, inflammation, cuts, grazes and burns.
OTHER USES: Massage, compress, creams, facial sauna, local washes, bath, sitz-bath, inhalant, fragrance burner, aerosol spray, personal perfume, scent balls.
PERFUMERY: Colognes, toilet waters, floral scents.

LATIN NAME: *Lavandula angustifolia*

TYPE OF PLANT: evergreen shrub

COUNTRY OF ORIGIN: Mediterranean

PART OF PLANT USED: flowering heads

METHOD OF EXTRACTION: steam distillation

MAJOR CONSTITUENTS: a complexity of esters, alcohols, terpenes, ketones and others

FRAGRANCE: sweet, herbaceous, slightly floral

GERANIUM

REGULATING

From a pelargonium, not a true geranium, the scent of this oil can be quite delightful. Here is the green balancer and harmonizer which is very useful for menopausal or premenstrual problems. An anti-depressant, geranium is a good remedy when you're feeling liverish. Mildly diuretic, it will help circulation and assist the body in releasing toxins.

PROPERTIES AND USES

EMOTIONAL: Anxiety, tension, depression, listlessness.
DIGESTIVE: Diarrhea, liver tonic.
MUSCULAR: Rheumatism.
CIRCULATORY: Fluid retention, edema, hemorrhoids, cellulite.
GENITO-URINARY: Urinary and vaginal infections, premenstrual syndrome, heavy periods, menopause.
SKIN CARE: Puffiness, acne, eczema, wounds, burns, nosebleed, mouthwash, insect repellant, deodorant.
OTHER USES: Massage, compress, creams, mouthwash, bath, sitz-bath, fragrance burner, aerosol spray, scent balls.
PERFUMERY: Scents, colognes, deodorants.

WARNING: There is a very slight risk of allergic reaction in some sensitive people.

LATIN NAME: *Pelargonium x asperum/Pelargonium graveolens* and other cultivars

TYPE OF PLANT: small shrub

COUNTRY OF ORIGIN: South Africa

PART OF PLANT USED: leaves

METHOD OF EXTRACTION: steam distillation

MAJOR CONSTITUENTS: alcohols (citronellol, geraniol, linalol) and others, depending on cultivar

FRAGRANCE: light, fresh, green, often with rosy undertones

PALMAROSA

CAPRICIOUS

A relative of vetiver and lemongrass, and used in its native land as a protection against fevers, this under-rated remedy will come to the rescue in times of influenza and high temperature, when stronger oils might be too stimulating. Combining a delightful fragrance with powerful healing properties, it is a gentle tonic for the entire system. In an aerosol in summer, it will keep the atmosphere light and clean, and in winter provides a contrast to more stimulating oils, such as eucalyptus or lemon. Palmarosa has many uses in sickness and skin care, and is a fragrance that can be fun to work with.

PROPERTIES AND USES

EMOTIONAL: Fatigue, nervous depression, shock.
RESPIRATORY: Bronchitis, sinusitis.
DIGESTIVE: Diarrhea, gastroenteritis.
MUSCULAR: Rheumatism, arthritis.
CIRCULATORY: Cardiac tonic.
GENITO-URINARY: Cystitis, thrush, premenstrual syndrome.
SKIN CARE: Fungal infections, eczema, acne, broken capillaries.
OTHER USES: Massage, creams, local washes, bath, sitz-bath, inhalant, fragrance burner, aerosol spray, personal perfume, scent balls.
PERFUMERY: Light and floral blends, colognes and deodorants.

LATIN NAME: *Cymbopogen martinii*

TYPE OF PLANT: flowering grass

COUNTRY OF ORIGIN: India

PART OF PLANT USED: fresh or dried grass

METHOD OF EXTRACTION: steam distillation

MAJOR CONSTITUENTS: alcohols (geraniol) ketones and terpenes

FRAGRANCE: sweet, floral, feminine

PETITGRAIN

EQUILIBRIUM

Petitgrain comes from the leaf of the bitter orange tree whose flowers produce the lovely neroli. It is a rather special oil. Its gift is to encourage mind and body to relax when in a persistent state of anxiety, and it may have a role to play in treating auto-immune diseases. Petitgrain balances rather than sedates. Its mild antiseptic and anti-spasmodic nature make it useful for a variety of digestive and respiratory problems, and it is a good skin tonic.

PROPERTIES AND USES

EMOTIONAL: Anxiety, apprehension, panic, opening-night nerves, shock.
RESPIRATORY: Minor infections, colds, influenza.
DIGESTIVE: Dyspepsia, nervous stomach, liver tonic.
MUSCULAR: Stress-induced pain and spasm.
CIRCULATORY: Tonic and cleansing, palpitations.
GENITO-URINARY: Premenstrual syndrome, menopause.
SKIN CARE: Puffiness, oily, acne, deodorant, scalp tonic.
OTHER USES: Massage, compress, creams, facial sauna, personal perfume, fragrance burner, inhalant, scent balls.
PERFUMERY: Scents, colognes, deodorants, air fresheners.

LATIN NAME: *Citrus aurantium ssp aurantium*

TYPE OF PLANT: evergreen tree

COUNTRY OF ORIGIN: Far East and Mediterranean

PART OF PLANT USED: leaves

METHOD OF EXTRACTION: steam distillation

MAJOR CONSTITUENTS: mainly esters (linalyl acetate and geranyl acetate), alcohols, terpenes and others

FRAGRANCE: fresh, piquant and floral with citrus undertones

JASMINE

SULTRY

Jasmine's waxy flowers open to the night air and should be harvested before dawn. Known as the king of oils, if only by virtue of its price, it is of great value when dealing with apathy, timidity, fear and paranoia, and many psychosomatic problems. As an aphrodisiac, jasmine helps to restore faith in one's sexuality, it is a great confidence-booster, and a wonderful perfume in its own right. The distillate can be used in skin care and is a uterine tonic, but its many other uses are perhaps better dealt with by far cheaper oils. Like rose, jasmine's exquisite scent is virtually impossible to imitate and well worth keeping as a treat for special occasions.

PROPERTIES AND USES

EMOTIONAL: Aphrodisiac, depression, apprehension, fear, paranoia, poor self-esteem, emotional coldness.
GENITO-URINARY: Impotence, frigidity, premenstrual syndrome, menopause, postnatal depression.
SKIN CARE: Dry, sensitive, improves elasticity.
PERFUMERY: Sweet, exotic blends.
OTHER USES: Massage, creams, personal perfume.

WARNING: Frequently adulterated, many cheap imitations of jasmine exist. There is a very slight risk of an allergic reaction.

LATIN NAME: *Jasminum officinale*

TYPE OF PLANT: evergreen shrub

COUNTRY OF ORIGIN: China

PART OF PLANT USED: flowers

METHOD OF EXTRACTION: solvent extraction and steam distillation

MAJOR CONSTITUENTS: esters, alcohols, and many others

FRAGRANCE: rich, creamy, and floral

NEROLI (ORANGE BLOSSOM)

REASSURANCE

Full of youthful loveliness, the delicate orange flower is a favorite for bridal bouquets, and the scent is tipped as an aphrodisiac. It has a soothing, slightly hypnotic quality and is very reassuring for people in a state of shock or suffering from nervous depression. Neroli is antibacterial, a digestive and phlebotonic, and the distillate is useful for every skin type. Its unsurpassed fragrance has made it a favorite ingredient of eau-de-colognes since its arrival in Europe in the 16th century.

PROPERTIES AND USES

EMOTIONAL: Depression, hysteria, shock, fatigue, nervous exhaustion, insomnia, anorexia.
RESPIRATORY: Breathlessness, loss of voice.
CIRCULATORY: Palpitations, varicose veins.
SKIN CARE: All types, promotes new cell growth.
OTHER USES: Massage, compress, creams, personal perfume, scent balls.
PERFUMERY: High-class perfumes and colognes.

WARNING: Many cheap imitations exist. Neroli is often adulterated with petitgrain.

LATIN NAME: *Citrus aurantium ssp aurantium*

TYPE OF PLANT: evergreen tree

COUNTRY OF ORIGIN: Far East and Mediterranean

PART OF PLANT USED: flowers

METHOD OF EXTRACTION: solvent extraction and steam distillation

MAJOR CONSTITUENTS: a complexity of alcohols, esters, ketones, and others

FRAGRANCE: enticingly sweet, soft and heady

ROSE

FEMININITY

A symbol of love and perfection, this delightful fragrance has been associated with all that is beautiful and noble. Rose oil is the supreme healer, a tonic and cleanser for the entire system with a nurturing effect which makes it of use in treating almost any long-standing condition. For grief, bereavement, and emotional wounds, this is the essence to reach for.

PROPERTIES AND USES

EMOTIONAL: Grief, loneliness, repressed anger, envy, resentment, impatience, confusion, shock.
RESPIRATORY: Mild infections, coughs and wheezing.
DIGESTIVE: Nausea, nervous stomach, anorexia, liver tonic.
GENITO-URINARY: Vaginal and urinary infections, period pains, pre-menstrual syndrome, menopause, postnatal depression, impotence, frigidity, uterine tonic.
SKIN CARE: All types, especially mature and sensitive.
CIRCULATORY: Tonic and cleansing.
OTHER USES: Massage, compress, local wash, creams, bath, sitz-bath, personal perfume, scent balls.
PERFUMERY: Fine fragrances and cosmetics.

NOTE: In most cases a distillate, or otto, is obtained from *Rosa damascena*, the damask rose, and an absolute from *Rosa centifolia*, the cabbage rose.

LATIN NAME: *Rosa damascena/Rosa centifolia*

TYPE OF PLANT: small flowering shrub

COUNTRY OF ORIGIN: Middle East and Orient

PART OF PLANT USED: petals

METHOD OF EXTRACTION: distillation and solvent extraction

MAJOR CONSTITUENTS: alcohols (citronellol, geraniol, nerol), esters, rose oxides, and others, depending on species

FRAGRANCE: soft, syrupy, green, and floral

YLANG YLANG

REJUVENATING

This "flower of flowers" is associated with weddings in its native land and often called poor man's jasmine. It is primarily an oil for the skin and nervous system, and is lovely in a face massage to relieve tension, clenched teeth, furrowed brows, and blotchy skin caused by stress. Ylang ylang can also regulate the breathing and heartbeat, and relieve frustration, rage, hysteria, panic, palpitations, and shock. It is useful for premenstrual syndrome, mood swings, and tension headaches (but in minute quantities; otherwise, it could have the reverse effect), general nervousness, and feelings of isolation. Popular in hair care, it can give extra sheen and fragrance.

PROPERTIES AND USES

EMOTIONAL: Mood swings, anger, anxiety, irritability, depression, impotence, frigidity.
DIGESTIVE: Nervous stomach.
CIRCULATORY: Palpitations, rapid heartbeat, hypertension.
SKIN CARE: All types, but especially oily, hair and scalp tonic.
OTHER USES: Massage, creams, bath, personal perfume.
PERFUMERY: Lends elegance to many blends.

WARNING: Use sparingly. A cheap oil can be sickly.
For best results, buy only ylang ylang extra.

LATIN NAME: *Canaga odorata*

TYPE OF PLANT: flowering tree

COUNTRY OF ORIGIN: Philippines

PART OF PLANT USED: flowers

METHOD OF EXTRACTION: steam distillation

MAJOR CONSTITUENTS: esters, alcohols, terpenes, and others

FRAGRANCE: intensely sweet, floral, creamy

BENZOIN

CUSHIONING

Benzoin's sweet smell is familiar as a constituent of friar's balsam. It first appeared in Europe as "gum benjamin" and was a favorite with England's Queen Elizabeth I, who had it powdered with another warm herb, sweet marjoram, as a perfume and skin softener. The oil is thick, brown, sticky, and protective. It will shift mucus, make a wonderful inhalant, and pamper the skin, especially when it is chapped and sore. Infused with the sun of its native habitat, benzoin brings comfort to the heart and spirits, and provides a soothing remedy, especially in wintertime.

PROPERTIES AND USES

EMOTIONAL: Frayed nerves, emotional wounds, lack of communication, grief, fear, withdrawal, general debility.
RESPIRATORY: Bronchitis, catarrh, coughs, colds, sore throats, pulmonary antiseptic.
MUSCULAR: Rheumatism, arthritis.
SKIN CARE: Chapped, dry, irritated, wounds, scars, promotes new cell growth.
OTHER USES: Massage, cream, fragrance burner, scent balls.

WARNING: Use sparingly. Possible skin sensitization. Benzoin can be soporofic in high doses.

LATIN NAME: *Styrax benzoe*

TYPE OF PLANT: large tree

COUNTRY OF ORIGIN: Tropical Asia

PART OF PLANT USED: resin

METHOD OF EXTRACTION: solvent extraction

MAJOR CONSTITUENTS: benzoic and cinnamic acid, vanillin

FRAGRANCE: sweet, vanilla-like

FRANKINCENSE

PROTECTIVE

Known as "olibanum" – oil of Lebanon – frankincense has a dignified history of spiritual healing, and as an offering to the baby Jesus, it was said to signify his priesthood. Frankincense is a popular incense and, like its cousin, myrrh, comes from a tough desert tree which secretes a resin when the bark is wounded. A rejuvenator for dull, aging skin, an expectorant and pulmonary antiseptic, it can deepen the breathing and help the immune response. Infused with the warm desert air, frankincense brings solace in times of weakness or bereavement, and is a valuable oil to treat any form of depression due to the onset of winter.

PROPERTIES AND USES

EMOTIONAL: Depression, obsession, debility, fear, paranoia, bereavement, insomnia, seasonal affective disorder.
RESPIRATORY: Bronchitis, catarrh, sinusitis, breathlessness.
GENITO-URINARY: Menopause, premenstrual syndrome.
SKIN CARE: Mature, stretch marks, scar tissue.
OTHER USES: Massage, creams, bath, inhalant, fragrance burner, aerosol spray.
PERFUMERY: Useful in many fragrances.

LATIN NAME: *Boswellia carterii*

TYPE OF PLANT: tree-like shrub

COUNTRY OF ORIGIN: Northeast Africa

PART OF PLANT USED: resin

METHOD OF EXTRACTION: steam distillation

MAJOR CONSTITUENTS: terpenes, alcohols, and others

FRAGRANCE: warm, sweet, light, and balsamic. A high-quality oil will often have subtle, lemon fragrance

MYRRH

OPENING AND DRYING

Myrrh comes from a resilient desert tree with a thick, fragrant bark which, when wounded, secretes resin as a protection against the desert sun. It is an ancient and respected wound healer and panacea for many diseases of the old world, such as dysentery and leprosy. Used in the Egyptian embalming process and valued spiritually for its perfume. Soothing, drying, and fortifying, myrrh has an antifungal quality and is useful in many skin, gum, and bronchial disorders. It has a steadying effect on the nerves.

PROPERTIES AND USES

EMOTIONAL: Relaxing and useful in meditation.
RESPIRATORY: Bronchitis, catarrh, coughs, sore throats.
DIGESTIVE: Diarrhea, colic.
GENITO-URINARY: Uterine tonic, vaginal thrush.
SKIN CARE: Cracked, chapped, mature, mouth and gum infections.
OTHER USES: Massage, compress, cream, mouthwash, sitz-bath, fragrance burner, scent balls.
PERFUMERY: A useful fixative in heavy, floral blends.

WARNING: Use sparingly. Avoid during pregnancy.

LATIN NAME: *Commiphora molmol/Commiphora myrrha*

TYPE OF PLANT: shrub-like tree

COUNTRY OF ORIGIN: North Africa and Asia

PART OF PLANT USED: resin

METHOD OF EXTRACTION: steam distillation

MAJOR CONSTITUENTS: terpenes, ketones, aldehydes, and others

FRAGRANCE: bitter-sweet, rich, resinous

BERGAMOT

REFRESHING

A popular Italian folk remedy, said to be a cross between a citrus and a pear – not authenticated, but easy to believe when one smells it – this lighthearted fragrance works primarily on the nervous system. It is also a good urinary antiseptic, and it is very useful in skin care, but preferably under supervision due to its photosensitivity. Anti-infectious and supremely uplifting, it makes a marvelous room spray in times of illness or depression, cleansing, deodorizing, and keeping insects away.

PROPERTIES AND USES

EMOTIONAL: Irritability, anxiety, hypertension, depression, exhaustion, insomnia, lack of confidence, mood swings.
RESPIRATORY: Aerial antiseptic.
DIGESTIVE: Loss of appetite, nausea, nervous stomach.
GENITO-URINARY: Cystitis and other urinary tract infections, pre-menstrual syndrome, menopause.
OTHER USES: Sitz-bath, fragrance burner, aerosol spray, scent balls.
PERFUMERY: Colognes, toilet waters, air fresheners.

WARNING: Bergamot is one of the most photosensitive of the citrus oils. If applied to the skin, do not sunbathe or use an ultraviolet lamp for at least 24 hours.

LATIN NAME: *Citrus aurantium ssp bergamia*

TYPE OF PLANT: small tree

COUNTRY OF ORIGIN: Tropical Asia, now cultivated in Italy

PART OF PLANT USED: rinds of the fruit

METHOD OF EXTRACTION: expression

MAJOR CONSTITUENTS: alcohols, esters, terpenes, and furo-coumarins

FRAGRANCE: fresh, sweetly citrus with a hint of pear

GRAPEFRUIT

AWAKENING

A very light, delicate oil and a good air ioniser. The fragrance of grapefruit is extremely uplifting and invigorating, and can help if you're feeling jaded, jet-lagged, or generally run-down. It is a helpful regulator for the digestion and a tonic for the liver and gall bladder. Antiseptic and good for the circulation, grapefruit can be a useful addition to a pre-exercise rub or as a local disinfectant in the locker room.

PROPERTIES AND USES

EMOTIONAL: Fatigue, listlessness, jet lag.
RESPIRATORY: Aerial antiseptic.
DIGESTIVE: Liverishness, nervous, stomach, erratic eating habits.
MUSCULAR: Muscle tone, local stimulation, stiffness, pre-and aprés-sport.
CIRCULATORY: Fluid retention, overweight.
SKIN CARE: Acne, oily, tonic and astringent, cellulite.
OTHER USES: Massage, fragrance burner, personal inhalant, aerosol spray.
PERFUMERY: Fresh, lighthearted blends.

WARNING: Grapefruit is photosensitive; do not sunbathe or use an ultraviolet lamp for at least 24 hours after applying to skin.

LATIN NAME: *Citrus x paradisii*

TYPE OF PLANT: tall tree

COUNTRY OF ORIGIN: Tropical Asia and West Indies

PART OF PLANT USED: rinds of fruit

METHOD OF EXTRACTION: expression

MAJOR CONSTITUENTS: terpenes, alcohols (paradisol, geraniol), aldehydes, furo-coumarins, and others

FRAGRANCE: light, refreshingly citrus

LEMON

SPARKLING

This natural spring cleaner has a talent for getting rid of stale smells, and its bright, clean fragrance immediately lifts the spirits, sharpens the brain, and acts as a liver tonic. The lemon tree loves light, and its oil is good for treating emotional conditions caused by a lack of it. It can purify and strengthen the circulation and help the body to ward off germs, viruses, and respiratory infections. Lemon has a use in skin care, but with the same precautions as for other citrus oils, and like them it is a valuable source of vitamin C.

PROPERTIES AND USES

EMOTIONAL: Tonic, stimulating, fatigue, listlessness, general debility.
RESPIRATORY: Colds, influenza, aerial disinfectant.
DIGESTIVE: Liver tonic, heartburn, over-acidity, hangover.
MUSCULAR: Gout, rheumatism, cramp.
SKIN CARE: Acne, oily, chilblains, tonic and astringent.
OTHER USES: Massage, compress, bath, fragrance burner, aerosol spray.

WARNING: Lemon is photosensitive. Do not sunbathe or use an ultra-violet lamp for at least 24 hours after applying to the skin. It may irritate a sensitive skin.

LATIN NAME: *Citrus limon*

TYPE OF PLANT: small evergreen tree

COUNTRY OF ORIGIN: Asia and Mediterranean

PART OF PLANT USED: rinds of fruits

METHOD OF EXTRACTION: expression

MAJOR CONSTITUENTS: terpenes, alcohols, esters, furo-coumarins, and others

FRAGRANCE: sharp, citrus, fresh, clean

ORANGE

JOYFUL

Used by Chinese and Arab physicians to treat melancholy, this is a remedy par excellence *to raise the spirits and encourage a festive atmosphere. It brings a light-hearted sense of well-being. In the wintertime, orange will be enhanced by a spice oil, and like other citruses, it can be useful for feelings of withdrawal due to the declining light. Orange is a good blood cleanser and helpful for calming sanguine personalities. It is a tonic for the digestive system and has a use in skin care.*

PROPERTIES AND USES

EMOTIONAL: Depression, anxiety, dizziness, convalescence, seasonal affective disorder.
RESPIRATORY: Airborne infections.
DIGESTIVE: Nervous stomach, travel sickness, flatulence.
CIRCULATORY: Tonic and decongestant, palpitations.
GENITO-URINARY: Premenstrual syndrome, menopause.
SKIN CARE: Softens and hydrates, scalp tonic.
OTHER USES: Massage, bath, fragrance burner, aerosol spray, scent balls.
PERFUMERY: Fresh, lively blends.

WARNING: Orange is photosensitive; do not sunbathe or use an ultraviolet lamp for at least 24 hours after applying to skin. It may irritate a sensitive skin.

LATIN NAME: *Citrus aurantium ssp aurantium*

TYPE OF PLANT: evergreen tree

COUNTRY OF ORIGIN: Far East and Mediterranean

PART OF PLANT USED: rinds of the fruit

METHOD OF EXTRACTION: expression

MAJOR CONSTITUENTS: mainly terpenes (limonene) and others, including furo-coumarins

FRAGRANCE: warm, tangy, citrus

CYPRESS

STRENGTHENING

From a beautiful, cone-shaped tree often growing in fragrant groves and a favorite windbreak, cypress has been used in Middle Eastern culture as a purifying and protective incense, and as a remedy it is useful in all conditions where there is a need for elasticity. Strengthening arteries, veins, weakened ligaments, and tissues, cypress is mildly constricting for the capillaries and has a balancing and restraining effect on body fluids. Likewise, for overstrained nerves, unrestrained weeping, and the inability to cope, its fragrance concentrates the mind.

PROPERTIES AND USES

EMOTIONAL: General fatigue and debility, fragmented thoughts, hopelessness, bereavement.
RESPIRATORY: Spasmodic coughs, bronchitis.
DIGESTIVE: Diarrhea, enteritis.
MUSCULAR: Cramp, overexertion.
CIRCULATORY: Cardiovascular problems, varicose veins, hemorrhoids, excessive perspiration, edema.
GENITO-URINARY: Cystitis, prostatitis, premenstrual syndrome, menopause, painful and heavy periods.
SKIN CARE: Tonic, astringent, deodorant, broken capillaries, cellulite.
OTHER USES: Massage, compress, bath, sitz-bath, fragrance burner, inhalant, personal perfume, aerosol spray.
PERFUMERY: Colognes, deodorants, and masculine scents.

LATIN NAME: *Cupressus sempervirens*

TYPE OF PLANT: evergreen tree

COUNTRY OF ORIGIN: Eastern Mediterranean

PART OF PLANT USED: needles, twigs, and sometimes cones

METHOD OF EXTRACTION: steam distillation

MAJOR CONSTITUENTS: terpenes, alcohols

FRAGRANCE: honey-sweet, woody, balsamic

JUNIPER BERRY

PURIFYING

Juniper branches burn brightly and have been used in purification rites for centuries. A cleansing and reviving remedy, good for any system that is sluggish and unable to eliminate toxins, **but care must be taken since it is a diuretic and may overstimulate the kidneys**. *It has a warming and analgesic effect, and is good for the local circulation, rheumatism, and gout. Its sharp, piquant scent is an emotional purifier. Brush a few drops of juniper berry oil through your hair to shake off unwanted vibrations at the end of a hard day.*

PROPERTIES AND USES

EMOTIONAL: Exhaustion, depletion, overwork, worry.
RESPIRATORY: Colds, influenza, airborne infections.
MUSCULAR: Arthritis, gout, rheumatism.
CIRCULATORY: Tonic and diuretic, aprés-sport.
GENITO-URINARY: Premenstrual syndrome, urinary infections.
SKIN CARE: Acne, oily, puffiness, cellulite.
OTHER USES: Massage, compress, bath, sitz-bath, facial sauna, inhalant, fragrance burner, aerosol.
PERFUMERY: Masculine notes.

WARNING: Use sparingly. Avoid juniper berry oil during pregnancy, kidney disease, and weaknesses.

LATIN NAME: *Juniperus communis*

TYPE OF PLANT: small, evergreen tree

COUNTRY OF ORIGIN: northern hemisphere

PART OF PLANT USED: berries

METHOD OF EXTRACTION: steam distillation

MAJOR CONSTITUENTS: terpenes, alcohols, and esters

FRAGRANCE: fresh, sweet, and fiery

SCOTS PINE

INVIGORATING

A walk in a natural pine forest is a wonderful experience, and the oil itself is cleansing and oxygenating, a real tonic, especially for the respiratory system. A tonic, too, for the circulation and lymph, scots pine oil can encourage the body to release toxins and is helpful for heavy smokers, those who lead sedentary lives, or who are convalescing. For colds, influenza, bronchitis, winter aches and pains, this remedy is invaluable.

PROPERTIES AND USES

EMOTIONAL: Nervous exhaustion, after influenza, lack of confidence, staying power, seasonal affective disorder.
RESPIRATORY: Bronchitis, sinusitis, coughs, wheezing, breathlessness, hayfever.
MUSCULAR: Rheumatism, gout, arthritis, stiffness, lumbago, neuralgia, pre- and aprés-sport.
CIRCULATORY: Tonic and decongestant, immuno-stimulant.
GENITO-URINARY: Urinary tract infections.
SKIN CARE: Fungal infections, deodorant, insect repellent.
OTHER USES: Massage, compress, bath, sitz-bath, inhalant, fragrance burner, aerosol spray, scent balls.
PERFUMERY: Masculine scents, deodorants.

WARNING: Scots pine oil can cause skin sensitization in certain people.

LATIN NAME: *Pinus sylvestris*

TYPE OF PLANT: tall, evergreen tree

COUNTRY OF ORIGIN: northern hemisphere

PART OF PLANT USED: needles

METHOD OF EXTRACTION: steam distillation

MAJOR CONSTITUENTS: mainly terpenes with alcohols, aldehydes, and other

FRAGRANCE: fresh, penetrating, and resinous

PEPPERMINT

REVIVING

Celebrated in Greek mythology, this popular digestive aid has special analgesic and anti-spasmodic properties which can relieve many stomach problems, headaches, or migraines associated with neuralgia, nausea, or sinusitis. It has expectorant and antiseptic qualities which make it useful during periods of colds and influenza, though it is not recommended as an inhalant except under supervision.

PROPERTIES AND USES

EMOTIONAL: Heatstroke, shock, general fatigue, nervousness.
RESPIRATORY: Colds, chills, sinusitis, airborne infections.
DIGESTIVE: Vomiting, nausea, stomach cramps, colic, hangover, travel sickness.
MUSCULAR: Cramps, pre- and aprés-sport.
CIRCULATORY: Cardiac tonic.
SKIN CARE: Mouthwash, bruises (under professional supervision).
OTHER USES: Local massage, compress, aerosol spray, personal inhalant, scent balls.

> WARNING: Avoid during pregnancy or in conjunction with homeopathic remedies. Do not use peppermint on small children, babies, sensitive skins, or late at night.

LATIN NAME: *Mentha piperita*

TYPE OF PLANT: fragrant herb

COUNTRY OF ORIGIN: Mediterranean

PART OF PLANT USED: leaves

METHOD OF EXTRACTION: steam distillation

MAJOR CONSTITUENTS: alcohols (menthol), esters, oxides, ketones, (menthone), terpenes

FRAGRANCE: cool, fresh, bitter-sweet, and minty

SANDALWOOD

LUBRICATING

One of the oldest known perfumes and still regarded as a sacred panacea, sandalwood comes from a fragrant wood used in the East for temple building. The thick, slightly sticky oil is balancing, lubricating, and useful in all types of skin care, especially where a natural antiseptic is needed. Wonderfully soothing for the nervous system, sandalwood can encourage aggressive people to become more relaxed personalities. This comforting and tenacious scent is the secret ingredient in many aphrodisiac blends.

PROPERTIES AND USES

EMOTIONAL: Insomnia and many stress related conditions, impotence, frigidity, anxiety, aggression, and egocentric behavior.
RESPIRATORY: Bronchitis, laryngitis, irritating coughs.
DIGESTIVE: Diarrhea, nausea.
MUSCULAR: Neuralgia, sciatica, lumbago.
CIRCULATORY: Cardiac fatigue, varicose veins, hemorrhoids.
GENITO-URINARY: Mild urinary tract and genital infections, impotence, frigidity, premenstrual syndrome.
SKIN CARE: Dry, oily, eczema, cracked, chapped, hair and scalp tonic.
OTHER USES: Massage, creams, bath, sitz-bath, gargle, fragrance burner, personal perfume, scent balls.
PERFUMERY: Many classic perfumes.

NOTE: Do not confuse with amyris (West Indian sandalwood).

LATIN NAME: *Santalum album*

TYPE OF PLANT: semi-parasitic tree

COUNTRY OF ORIGIN: India

PART OF PLANT USED: heartwood

METHOD OF EXTRACTION: steam distillation

MAJOR CONSTITUENTS: mainly alcohols (santalols), acids, and terpenes

FRAGRANCE: warm, woody, sweet, and sensuous

PATCHOULI

LINGERING

A traditional aphrodisiac perfume, and popular as part of the sixties Flower Power culture, a good-quality oil is a lovely amber color with a rich, intensely lingering fragrance. Its effect on the senses is, surprisingly, not sedative, rather more balancing and uplifting and, if overused, it may even prevent sleep. Patchouli is an excellent deodorant, especially in hot, humid conditions, and in skin care, it can heal cracked or infected skin. It is known to have a tonic and antiseptic effect on the colon and has been of use in treating constipation and infectious diarrhea, especially in hot climates.

PROPERTIES AND USES

EMOTIONAL: Depression, impotence, frigidity, nervous exhaustion, lethargy.
RESPIRATORY: Airborne infections.
SKIN CARE: Cracked or chapped, acne, eczema, dermatitis, fungal infections, insect repellent, cellulite.
DIGESTIVE: Constipation, diarrhea.
OTHER USES: Massage, creams, bath, fragrance burner, aerosol spray, personal perfume, scent balls.
PERFUMERY: Gives a base to many different blends.

LATIN NAME: *Pogostomon cablin*

TYPE OF PLANT: bushy herb

COUNTRY OF ORIGIN: Indonesia

PART OF PLANT USED: young, dried, and fermented leaves

METHOD OF EXTRACTION: steam distillation

MAJOR CONSTITUENTS: alcohols (patchoulol), ketones, acids, and others

FRAGRANCE: rich, sweet, earthy

VETIVER

GROUNDING

A complex and interesting oil, useful whenever there is a need to bring someone down to earth. It helps to put us back in touch with Mother Earth and shows us the division we have created between mind and body. Useful for nervous personalities and those who tend to live in a world of fantasy. Under professional supervision, it has a use in skin care, can be a tonic to the liver, glands, and circulation, and is a good immuno-stimulant, having a generally strengthening effect on the system. Vetiver is an excellent insect repellent; the grass is woven into mats and blinds to keep away moths and bugs in its native land.

PROPERTIES AND USES

EMOTIONAL: Stabilizing, grounding, protective, sedative, depression, debility, exhaustion, lack of interest.
PERFUMERY: Insect repellent, masculine scents and colognes.
OTHER USES: Fragrance burner, aerosol spray, personal perfume, scent balls.

NOTE: Vetiver is often adulterated.

LATIN NAME: *Vetiveria zizanoides*

TYPE OF PLANT: fragrant grass

COUNTRY OF ORIGIN: Indonesia

PART OF PLANT USED: roots

METHOD OF EXTRACTION: steam distillation

MAJOR CONSTITUENTS: terpenes, alcohols (vetiverol), esters, ketones

FRAGRANCE: rich, warm, and very earthy

THE REMEDIES

The following is a list of remedies using essential oils:

FIRST AID

Insect bites and stings, shock and fainting, minor burns, sprained ankle, minor cuts and grazes

AT HOME

Kitchen, bathroom, study, living room, bedroom

AT WORK

Frozen shoulder, writer's cramp, laryngitis, housemaid's knee, office ionizer

WORKING OUT

Sports and dance warm-up, après-sport cool down, cramp, athlete's foot, tennis elbow

SOCIAL EMBARRASSMENTS

Body odor, snoring, bad breath, hangover, flatulence

SEASONAL AILMENTS

Hayfever, heatstroke, sunburn, seasonal affective disorder, common cold

WOMEN

Cystitis, thrush, premenstrual syndrome, menopause

CHILDREN

Nosebleed, hiccups, asthma, colic, earache, hyperactivity

SKIN PROBLEMS

Eczema, cellulite, acne, broken capillaries, chapped hands

SOCIALIZING

Atmospheric blends for diffusers and fragrance burners, personal perfumes

FIRST AID

INSECT BITES AND STINGS

PREVENTION: Regular use of essential oils can be a general deterrent, and the following selection will keep the atmosphere fresh and provide a gentle alternative to harsher fly sprays.

ATTACK: If you **do** get bitten, resist the temptation to scratch and keep the area as cool as possible.

AEROSOL SPRAY

1 cup spring water
30–40 drops essential oils

For the essential oils, choose from geranium, lavender, eucalyptus citriodora, eucalyptus blue gum, myrtle, bergamot, rosemary, cypress, patchouli. Shake mixture well before use.

COMPRESS

1 cup spring water
1 drop geranium or chamomile
1 drop lavender

Use this compress as necessary to relieve pain. Blend together in the above proportions.

DABBING LOTION

1 drop geranium
1 drop lavender
1 drop tea tree

Dilute the above mixture in 1½ teaspoons witch hazel. Shake well. Use a cotton swab and dab onto the affected area.

SHOCK AND FAINTING

This is caused by a sudden and temporary loss of blood to the brain. Lay the person down with feet slightly raised, keep warm, and loosen tight clothing; hold a bottle of peppermint under their nose. **Send for medical help.** Pinch or slap hands until consciousness is regained. Massage hands and feet and encourage the patient to sit up, so that the head can be dropped between the knees if another attack comes on. Gently massage the temples and give them hot lemon and honey to drink. Later give the person a warm Bath, followed by a stomach Massage before bed.

INHALE

Peppermint, lavender or neroli

Use straight from the bottle.

BATH

1 drop chamomile
1 drop neroli
1 drop lavender

Mix together in these proportions.

MASSAGE

1 drop lavender
1 drop palmarosa or neroli
1 drop geranium

Dilute the above mixture in 1½ teaspoons almond oil.

WARNING: It is always advisable to call for medical help in the first instance.

MINOR BURNS

Apply undiluted lavender immediately; cover with gauze as above. Once the area starts to heal, add one or two drops of any of the following to a small amount of calendula cream and apply regularly: chamomile, geranium, palmarosa, lavender, benzoin, patchouli, sandalwood, frankincense, rose.

SPRAINED ANKLE

A sprain can occur around any joint and is caused by over-stretching or tearing a ligament. It is extremely painful and is generally accompanied by swelling. Support the ankle in an elevated position with a large pad of cotton and apply ice (a bag of frozen peas is good). Then apply cold Compresses (see below) at ten to fifteen-minute intervals for a couple of hours. **Do not put pressure on the area.** In due course the swelling should subside. Once the injury has healed, use the Massage below two or three times a day for a few days.

COMPRESS

1 cup cold water
2 drops chamomile
2 drops geranium

Blend together in the above proportions.

MASSAGE

1 drop sweet marjoram
1 drop black pepper
1 drop rosemary
1 drop lavender

Dilute all the above in 2 teaspoons of sweet almond oil.

WARNING: If symptoms do not subside, treat as a fracture and seek medical help immediately.

MINOR CUTS AND GRAZES

STEP ONE: Wash with clear, running water and then clean with a Local Wash made from a cupful of boiled and cooled water to which you have added two drops of lavender and two drops of tea tree.

STEP TWO: Apply undiluted lavender.

STEP THREE: Put two drops of lavender or geranium onto a piece of gauze and cover the wound, replacing two or three times a day.

AT HOME

Essential oils can be very useful around the house. Many are highly antiseptic and bactericidal, and can do a good job of cleaning, deodorizing, and generally enhancing the atmosphere.
Here are a few suggestions:

KITCHEN

As a cheap and practical alternative to more abrasive cleaners or sprays, try the following:

ALL PURPOSE CLEANER

10 drops lemon
10 drops grapefruit
10 drops petitgrain
10 drops tea tree
10 drops sandalwood

Keep the above mixture in a dropper bottle and add three or four drops to a basin of water when cleaning work surfaces, floors, and walls.

AEROSOL SPRAY

Choose from lemon, bergamot, cypress, petitgrain, myrtle, rosemary, sandalwood, peppermint, and pine oils.

Blend 30–40 drops chosen from four of the above oils in 1 cup of distilled water. Spray around to soak up stale smells.

FABRIC CONDITIONER RINSE

3 drops palmarosa
3 drops lavender

Blend and add to your final rinse, especially for whites or underwear.

Bathroom

Essential oils have many uses here. A few drops of pine make an excellent disinfectant, or for a more personal cosmetic touch try the following:

Scented Soap

8 oz bar unscented soap
2 drops sandalwood
4 drops palmarosa
1 drop patchouli
1 drop lemon (optional)

Grate the soap and put into the top of a double boiler. Dissolve slowly over gentle heat. Remove to cool. Add essential oils just as it begins to set. Mix thoroughly and pour into small molds.

Aftershave

2 drops palmarosa or petitgrain
1 drop coriander or eucalyptus

Blend the above in 1 cup of distilled water with 1 teaspoon of cider vinegar added. Shake well before use.

Study

Certain oils are effective aids when it comes to keeping one's brain alert; use sparingly however or you may achieve the reverse effect.

Working Late

2 drops lemon
2 drops coriander
1 drop black pepper
2 drops petitgrain or rosemary

Placed in a fragrance burner, this mixture will keep you alert until the early hours.

Scented Notepaper

Experiment with your favorite scents and add a personal touch to your letters. Make sure you use the oils that do not stain. Petitgrain, geranium, black pepper, coriander, lavender, and palmarosa are good ones, but there are many more.

LIVING ROOM

As a welcome and versatile alternative to synthetic fragrancers, essential oils can be very useful here:

AEROSOL SPRAY

5 drops each orange, grapefruit, bergamot, petitgrain, palmarosa, 3 drops each black pepper, sandalwood

Blend in 1 cup of distilled water. Spray a small amount onto carpets and curtains occasionally to keep them fresh.

POTPOURRIS

Add a couple of drops of oil to enliven your favorite potpourri. Choose from geranium, petitgrain, palmarosa, sandalwood, patchouli, benzoin, ylang ylang, orange, or lemon.

BEDROOM

A subtle blend of relaxing or romantic oils can be a valuable mood enhancer, but here, too, they have a practical application.

MOTHBALLS

lavender
geranium
palmarosa
patchouli
vetiver

A few drops, chosen from the above, dropped onto cotton balls and placed in closets and linen drawers should keep the moths at bay.

BEDLINEN/DRAWERS

Put a couple of your favorite oils onto sheets, pillowcases, or drawer liners.

AT WORK

FROZEN SHOULDER

This injury can set in after a pulled or overworked muscle has been ignored. There may be pain, restriction in arm movement, accompanied by a stiff neck, especially first thing in the morning. The condition could be made worse by stress and tension: driving with the car window open, sitting in a draft, or spending too many hours at a typewriter or word processor. Stretching exercises will help, accompanied by warm Compresses and regular, deep Massages, see below.

COMPRESS

1 cup warm water
2 drops marjoram
1 drop clary sage

Blend oils together in the above proportions.

MASSAGE

1 drop marjoram
1 drop clary sage
1 drop black pepper or ginger
1 drop lavender

Dilute the above oils in 2 teaspoons of sweet almond oil.
Keep area warm and draft-free at all times and avoid pressure, such as a heavy shoulder bag.

WRITER'S CRAMP

Anyone who has to keep their hand, or hands, in one position for long periods risks this condition. It is a really bad form of cramp which, if neglected, could involve pressure on nerves in the wrist leading to pain and tingling, similar to that of Carpal Tunnel syndrome.The best immediate treatment is Massage, see below, but a look at vitamin and mineral deficiency is also advisable.

Massage

2 drops cypress
1 drop geranium
1 drop rosemary

Dilute the above in 2 teaspoons of sweet almond oil. Putting the hand into a bowl of warm water with one or two drops of rosemary added can also help relieve the pain and tingling.

Laryngitis

Inflammation of the larynx or voice box. It can be an aftereffect of cold or influenza, or can be caused by polluted or smoky atmospheres, or simply by talking too much. Symptoms are loss of voice and difficulty swallowing, and the best advice is to rest, accompanied by steam Inhalations, Gargles, and Massage to the neck area. Take drinks made with fresh lemon and honey.

Steam Inhalation

1 drop benzoin or sandalwood
1 drop chamomile
1 drop lavender

Add oils to a bowl of hot water.

Massage

1 drop chamomile
1 drop pine or cypress
1 drop lavender

Dilute the above oils in 2 teaspoons of macadamia nut oil or St. John's wort oil.

Gargle

1 cup warm water
2–3 drops sandalwood

Warning: If symptoms persist, seek medical advice immediately.

Housemaid's Knee

This painful condition affects elbows and other joints, as well as knees, and is caused by repeated pressure on the area resulting in inflammation of the bursa, a protective sac around the joint.

Massage is not advisable at first, but an ice pack, accompanied by rest and followed up with alternate hot and cold Compresses, should help the swelling. Once the condition has started to heal, regular Massages and padding around the vulnerable area could prevent reoccurrences.

Compress

1 cup spring water
2 drops eucalyptus globulus
1 drop chamomile
1 drop peppermint

Mix together in these proportions.

Massage

2 drops lavender
1 drop rosemary
1 drop eucalyptus globulus

Dilute the above in 2 teaspoons of St. John's wort herbal oil

Office Ionizer

To create more negative ions and soak up smoke and sweat, try some of the following recipes. Experiment and see which combinations work best.

Sweat and Smoke Eliminantor

1 cup spring water
30–40 drops essential oils

Choose from five of the following: lemon, grapefruit, bergamot, pine, juniper, eucalyptus citriodora, palmarosa, honey myrtle, patchouli, geranium. Shake well before use.

General Atmosphere Freshener

1 cup spring water
30–40 drops essential oils

Choose from four or five of the following: orange, bergamot, rosemary, coriander, eucalyptus globulus and citriodora, geranium, palmarosa, lavender, petitgrain (and black pepper sparingly). Shake well before use.

Phone Freshener

Place a drop of tea tree and lavender on a cotton ball. Use it to wipe the mouthpiece regularly.

WORKING OUT

SPORTS AND DANCE WARM-UP

It is a good idea to tone up your muscles before exercise to improve the circulation. You can do this by brief, but vigorous massage, followed by a brisk rub with a cloth or towel.

WARM UP (NORMAL SKIN)

1 drop rosemary
2 drops pine
1 drop black pepper

Dilute the above in 2 teaspoons of sweet almond oil.

WARM UP (SENSITIVE SKIN)

1 drop lavender
2 drops cypress
1 drop palmarosa

Dilute in 2 teaspoons sweet almond oil.

APRÈS-SPORT COOL DOWN

Muscles should be given the opportunity to rest and detoxify after exercise, especially if you are not used to it. The fibers will want to shorten again after their exertion, and this is a good way to keep them supple and avoid cramps or more serious problems.

COOL DOWN

2 drops cypress
1 drop eucalyptus globulus
1 drop lavender
1 drop coriander or lemon

Dilute in 2 teaspoons of sweet almond oil.
Note: Drink plenty of spring water and relax, wrapped in a towel, for 20 minutes afterward.

APRÈS-SPORT RELAXING BATH

1 drop sandalwood
2 drops orange
1 drop clary sage

CRAMP

A distressingly painful condition usually affecting the calf muscle. It can be caused by impaired circulation, salt deficiency, or simply unaccustomed exercise.

ATTACK: A vigorous Massage along the length of the muscle.
PREVENTION: A regular pre-exercise massage is very helpful.

ATTACK MASSAGE

Choose from: rosemary, sweet marjoram, black pepper, ginger. Blend two drops in a two or three percent dilution with sweet almond oil.

PREVENTION MASSAGE

Choose from: rosemary, pine, coriander, eucalyptus globulus, cypress, lavender, palmarosa. Blend two or three drops in a two or three percent dilution with sweet almond oil.

WARNING: If symptoms persist, seek medical advice on diet and supplements.

ATHLETE'S FOOT

A highly contagious fungal infection encouraged by sweaty feet and often picked up in a changing room or moist environment, such as the edge of a swimming pool or jacuzzi.

ATTACK: Be sure to wash hands and clean nails immediately after touching the infection and keep footwear clean and well aired.

MASSAGE

3 drops tea tree
1 drop lavender

Mix oils thoroughly in a small cup of aloe vera gel or calendula cream, and apply to affected area.

MASSAGE

1 drop patchouli or myrrh
1 drop lemon
1 drop lavender

Mix oils thoroughly in a small cup of aloe vera gel or calendula cream, and apply to affected area.

PREVENTION Wear rubber sandals in the dressing room or around the swimming bath. At other times, keep feet as cool and dry as possible.

MASSAGE

2 drops tea tree
2 drops geranium

Blend in 2 teaspoons of calendula oil. Massage feet regularly.

Note: Always use your own towels and keep feet thoroughly dry and well ventilated. Where possible, wear open-toed sandals. Avoid man-made fibers and plastic shoes.

TENNIS ELBOW

Caused by excessive strain of muscles or tendons surrounding the elbow, due to sporting activities, regular lifting, or strenuous manual work. Often accompanied by Bursitis, inflammation, and swelling of the protective pad around the joint, a condition similar to Housemaid's Knee. The best treatment is rest, with an immediate ice pack if there is swelling, followed by alternate warm and cold Compresses. Once the pain starts to subside, Massage regularly.

COMPRESS

1 cup spring water
1 drop peppermint
1 drop eucalyptus globulus
2 drops lavender

If swelling is severe, substitute chamomile for eucalyptus.

MASSAGE

1 drop rosemary
1 drop cypress
1 drop black pepper (optional)
1 drop lavender

Dilute in 2 teaspoons St. John's wort oil. Massage around the immediately affected area, and continue with deep strokes down the forearm and into the hand. A regular massage is a good prevention if you are prone to this condition.

SOCIAL EMBARRASSMENTS

BODY ODOR

Normally this is a temporarily embarrassing nuisance, but if it persists, it may be a sign of hormonal imbalance or severe emotional disturbance. There are lots of deodorant oils which lend themselves successfully to Baths, Massages, and Aromatic Waters. Here are a few suggestions:

DEODORANT BATH

2 drops pine
2 drops lavender
1 drop geranium
1 drop lemon

Blend together in these proportions.

AFTER-BATH BODY OIL

2 drops sandalwood
2 drops cypress
2 drops petitgrain
2 drops lavender

Dilute the oils in 4 teaspoons of sweet almond oil.

AROMATIC WATER

Make your own, using the method described on page 11.

Choose from: lavender, cypress, rosemary, palmarosa, petitgrain, sandalwood, lemon, grapefruit, pine, peppermint, geranium, patchouli, frankincense, coriander, or ylang ylang.

SNORING

The old-fashioned method of sewing a pebble into the back of the pyjamas or nightdress to prevent the sufferer from lying on his or her back is still efficient. A temporary cause of snoring can be noisy breathing due to a cold or congestion. A steam Inhalation and a Chest Rub just before bed might help, as might a bowl of hot water by the radiator.

Steam Inhalation

1 drop benzoin
1 drop sweet marjoram or cypress
1 drop lavender

Add to a bowl of hot water.

Bowl of Water

3 drops pine
3 drops cypress
2 drops frankincense

Blend into a bowl of hot water.

Chest Rub

1 drop frankincense
2 drops honey myrtle
1 drop pine

Dilute in 2 teaspoons of sweet almond oil.

WARNING: Asthmatics should be cautious wherever steam is used.

Bad Breath

Another embarrassing condition, otherwise known as halitosis, it may be caused by stress, upset stomach, tooth decay, or simply what you had for dinner.

Bad Breath Gargle

1 cup boiled, cooled water
1 drop myrrh

Do not swallow.

Bad Breath Standby

Chew a couple of cardamom or coriander seeds, or a leaf of fresh mint.

Bad Breath Stomach

1 drop cardamom
1 drop orange
1 drop neroli

Diluted in $1\frac{1}{2}$ teaspoons of sweet almond oil. Massage in a clockwise direction just above the navel.

HANGOVER

Only time can really cure that morning-after feeling, but here are a few temporary measures. Drink lots of spring water and fresh orange juice or water with a slice of fresh lemon in it, and eat (if you can manage it) a bowl of live yogurt. Try the following:

MORNING-AFTER BATH

1 drop rosemary
1 drop lemon or juniper
2 drops grapefruit
1 drop sandalwood

MORNING-AFTER COMPRESS

1 cup spring water
2 drops palmarosa or petitgrain
1 drop lavender
1 drop peppermint

Apply to forehead and back of neck.

MORNING-AFTER GARGLE

1 cup boiled, cooled water
2 drops geranium

Do not swallow.

STANDBY: PERSONAL INHALANTS:

Choose from: ginger, peppermint, lemon, rosemary, grapefruit, coriander.

FLATULENCE

Excessive stomach gas can be caused by eating habits, stress, infection, or breathing patterns – air always has to go somewhere. Relaxing and breathing more slowly and deeply will help, and if you suffer from pain and distension, try a clockwise Massage around the abdomen.

MASSAGE

1 drop cardamom
1 drop peppermint or black pepper
1 drop orange

Dilute in 1½ teaspoons of sweet almond oil.

MASSAGE

2 drops sweet marjoram
2 drops coriander

Dilute in 1½ teaspoons of sweet almond oil.

SEASONAL AILMENTS

SPRING

HAYFEVER

Swollen eyelids, runny nose, sneezing – the familiar symptoms of hayfever (inflammation of the mucus membranes of the nose) are usually caused by an allergic reaction to something, although they may be a side-effect of a cold. Tests should identify the offending allergen; meanwhile, aromatic Baths, Inhalations, Compresses, and Local Massage can help to relieve symptoms.

BATH

2 drops lavender
1 drop chamomile
1 drop lemon or geranium

COMPRESS/MASSAGE

1 cup cold water
2 drops lavender
1 drop chamomile or peppermint

Place on the bridge of the nose and change frequently. This blend can also be used to massage around the sinus area, behind ears, and down the sides of the neck.

STEAM/PERSONAL INHALATION

1 drop cypress or pine
1 drop myrtle
1 drop peppermint

Inhale over a bowl of hot water or straight from a handkerchief.

WARNING: Asthmatics should beware of inhalations.

SUMMER

HEATSTROKE

Intense heat is dangerous for anyone not properly adapted to it and may result in shivering, fainting – even collapse. There may be loss of salt due to excessive perspiration.

This is a serious condition. Send for medical help immediately. Meanwhile, lie the person down in a cool, dimly lit room. Sponge down, wrap them in a cold sheet, and give them salt water to drink. Apply cold Compresses to head and wrists.

SPONGE BATH

1 cup lukewarm water
3 drops eucalyptus globulus
3 drops lavender

COMPRESS

1 cup lukewarm water
2 drops eucalyptus globulus
1 drop peppermint

SUNBURN

Minor sunburn simply causes reddening and slight pain. More seriously, the skin can blister. Move to a cool place immediately, take a lukewarm Bath, and then apply a Lotion. Keep an Aerosol Spray handy as a standby.

BATH

2 drops lavender
2 drops chamomile

LOTION

1½ tablespoons aloe vera gel
1½ tablespoons St. John's wort oil
4 drops chamomile
8 drops lavender
4 drops geranium

AEROSOL SPRAY

1 cup spring water
50 drops lavender

WARNING: If you have no lotion, live yogurt is a useful substitute. If the condition is serious, treat as a proper burn and consult your doctor.

AUTUMN

SEASONAL AFFECTIVE DISORDER

The clocks are going back, the nights are drawing in – and you're feeling SAD. Seasonal affective disorder, or "sunlight starvation," can bring a profound sense of isolation and hopelessness – sufferers just wish they could hibernate. "Bright Light Therapy," using a daylight lamp, may be enhanced by the use of essential oils in the form of Baths, Perfumes, Diffusers, and Massage. Here are a few suggestions:

A HEALING BATH

1 drop rose otto
1 drop orange
1 drop grapefruit
2 drops geranium or pine

AFTER-BATH BODY OIL

2 drops petitgrain
2 drops ylang ylang
2 drops orange
2 drops sandalwood
1 drop frankincense

Dilute in 4 teaspoons of sweet almond oil.

FRAGRANCE BURNER/DIFFUSER/AEROSOL SPRAY

Choose from:

Orange, grapefruit, lemon, bergamot, palmarosa, pine, cypress, myrtle, frankincense, or ginger.

PERSONAL PERFUME

2 drops jasmine

Undiluted on wrists or behind ears.

WINTER

COMMON COLD

First signs are usually a sore throat, shivering, sneezing, aching head, and muscles. Go straight to bed, rest as much as possible, and drink lots of spring water. Aromatic Baths, Inhalations, and Chest Rubs will help to speed recovery.

BATH

2 drops tea tree
1 drop eucalyptus globulus
1 drop lemon

STEAM INHALATION

1 drop myrtle
1 drop rosemary
1 drop benzoin

Blend in a bowl of hot water.

FRAGRANCE BURNER/DIFFUSER/ AEROSOL SPRAY

Choose from:

Eucalyptus globulus or citriodora, lemon, black pepper, pine, cypress, tea tree, honey, myrtle, frankincense, palmarosa, rosemary, or lavender.

CHEST RUB

2 drops eucalyptus globulus
1 drop honey myrtle
1 drop sweet marjoram or ginger
1 drop frankincense

Dilute in 1 tablespoon of sweet almond oil.

WARNING: If high temperature persists, seek medical advice. Never use essential oils instead of prescribed medication.

WOMEN

CYSTITIS

Infection and/or inflammation of the bladder, causing a frequent desire to pass urine and a burning pain when doing so. Keep the area as clean as possible; always wipe from front to back. Drink lots of spring water, but no tea, coffee or alcohol, and keep your abdomen warm. Regular Sitz-baths, accompanied by Massages and Local Washes, will help.

SITZ-BATH

2 drops sandalwood
2 drops bergamot or chamomile
2 drops lavender

Use two or three times a day.

LOCAL WASH

3½ tablespoons cooled, boiled water
2 drops chamomile
2 drops bergamot or tea tree
3 drops lavender

Shake mixture well, soak cotton balls in solution, and swab around area after urinating.

MASSAGE

2 drops sandalwood
1 drop chamomile
1 drop juniper

Dilute in 2 teaspoons of sweet almond oil. Massage lower back and abdomen two or three times a day.

WARNING: If neglected, this can lead to a more serious condition, so if symptoms persist, seek medical help.

THRUSH

A fungal infection which thrives in moist, warm conditions and usually affects the mouth or the vagina. It can be sexually transmitted, but may also occur after a prolonged course of antibiotics or as an irritating side-effect of the contraceptive pill.

VAGINAL THRUSH

SITZ-BATH

2 drops tea tree
2 drops lavender
1 drop rose otto or geranium

Use two or three times a day.

ORAL THRUSH

MOUTHWASH

1 cup warm water
2 drops tea tree
or 1 drop myrrh

Rinse mouth two or three times a day. **Do not swallow.**

WARNING: Avoid synthetic underwear, eat plenty of live yogurt, and reduce the sugar level in your diet. If symptoms persist, seek medical advice.

PREMENSTRUAL SYNDROME

A term used to describe a variety of physical and emotional upsets that may arise during the week before a period. PMS is usually related to hormonal disturbances and increased fluid retention at this time. Symptoms vary enormously, ranging from headaches, depression, and mood swings to painful breasts, edema, and general puffiness. **The best course of action is to visit a qualified aromatherapist.**

Meanwhile, here are a few suggestions:

A RELAXING, DETOXIFYING BATH

1 drop juniper
2 drops geranium
1 drop ylang ylang

ABDOMEN MASSAGE TO RELIEVE PAIN AND DISTENTION

1 drop clary sage
1 drop chamomile
2 drops lavender

Dilute in 2 teaspoons of sweet almond oil.

A PERSONAL PERFUME TO GIVE YOU BACK YOUR HEART

2 drops rose absolute
2 drops neroli (optional)
4 drops lavender
4 drops petitgrain or orange
1 drop benzoin

Dilute in 4 teaspoons of jojoba or coconut oil, or using the method described in the introduction, see page 11.

A FRAGRANCE BURNER TO BANISH GLOOM

2 drops bergamot
1 drop lemon
1 drop petitgrain
1 drop rosemary
1 drop peppermint

MENOPAUSE

The "change of life" usually comes between the ages of 45 and 55, and is a time when the ovaries produce less estrogen, periods gradually cease, and the female body adjusts to a new hormonal balance. For some women, this is a time of rejuvenation and release, but others may experience fatigue, depression, and a sense of hopelessness. Classic symptoms include hot flushes, dizziness, and palpitations. There are many essential oils that can come to the rescue. Here are a few suggestions.

HOT FLUSHES: STANDBY

Keep a bottle of lavender permanently in your pocket and use to dab on forehead, temples, nape of neck, and wrists when an attack comes on. You could also use a cooling aromatic water – see recipe, page 11.

HOT FLUSHES: BATH AND MASSAGE FORMULA 1

2 drops cypress
2 drops geranium
1 drop clary sage or chamomile

Massage blend diluted in 2 teaspoons of sweet almond oil.

PALPITATIONS: STANDBY

Splash your wrists with cold water, or fill a bowl, add a couple of drops of ylang ylang and geranium, and place your hands and wrists in it. Inhale lavender and chamomile on a tissue. Massage your solar plexus area regularly with a three percent dilution of either lavender, chamomile, or neroli.

HOT FLUSHES: BATH AND MASSAGE FORMULA 2

2 drops cypress
2 drops palmarosa
2 drops sandalwood

Massage blend diluted in 2 teaspoons of sweet almond oil.

A COOLING PERSONAL PERFUME

2 drops jasmine
4 drops palmarosa
4 drops grapefruit
1 or 2 drops patchouli or sandalwood

Dilute in 1 tablespoon of jojoba or coconut oil, or use the method described on page 11.

CHILDREN

NOSEBLEED

Loosen clothing and sit with head slightly forward. Get the sufferer to breathe through the mouth.
Pinch the soft part of the nose slightly and apply a small cold Compress. Leave it there for five or ten minutes.

COMPRESS

1 cup cold water
1 drop lavender
1 drop geranium

WARNING: If the bleeding persists or is caused by an injury, send for medical help. Nosebleeds can sometimes be a sign of a more serious condition, such as high blood pressure.

HICCUPS

The old trick of dropping something cold down the back of the neck sometimes works, but the best method is an updated, aromatic version of the brown paper bag.

RECIPE

Put one drop of lavender or one drop of orange into a paper bag. Hold it over the mouth and nose, and get the sufferer to take between ten and twenty deep breaths.

ASTHMA

Great care should be taken over the use of essential oils by asthmatics, since some may cause allergic reactions in sensitive individuals, especially children. Use only the best oils. Beware also of the use of steam. It may not help if there is spasm and restriction in the upper respiratory tract. Oils which have proved to be useful for adults include: cypress, lavender, geranium, marjoram, frankincense, eucalyptus, peppermint, chamomile, ylang ylang, and neroli.

If an attack comes on unexpectedly, send for medical help. Meanwhile: Sit them upright in a stable position with elbows resting on a table or back of a chair so that the rib cage is raised slightly. Keep warm, perhaps with a hot water bottle on the chest, and gently massage upward along each side of the spine. Give them one of the above oils to inhale from a handkerchief.

WARNING: For children under eight, use only geranium or lavender. Never use essential oils instead of prescribed medication.

COLIC

A warm Compress, followed by a gentle abdomen Massage.

COMPRESS

1 cup warm water
1 drop chamomile
1 drop lavender

Place compress over lower abdomen, changing when necessary, for about ten minutes.

MASSAGE

1 drop lavender
1 drop orange
1 drop cardamom or coriander (optional)

Dilute in 2 teaspoons of sweet almond oil.
Massage in a clockwise direction for five minutes, or until pain subsides.

WARNING: For children under seven, use only lavender.

EARACHE

The ear is very delicate, so do not try to put essential oils inside, unless under professional supervision. However, for pain caused by a cold or a mild infection, a warm Compress will often ease pain. Another useful method is a gentle Massage around the outside of the ear.

COMPRESS

1 cup warm water
1 drop chamomile

MASSAGE

1 drop sweet marjoram
1 drop lavender

Dilute in 1 teaspoon of gently warmed sweet almond oil and massage around the back of the ear.

HYPERACTIVITY

Fast foods and food allergies are becoming acknowledged as major offenders, and advice should be sought. Meanwhile Massage on either the back, abdomen, hands, or feet just before bed, together with a diffuser in the bedroom, might help.

Choose from: Chamomile, lavender, petitgrain, neroli, palmarosa, or geranium.

WARNING: For Massage, use only a two or three percent dilution in sweet almond oil. If the child is under seven, use only lavender.

SKIN PROBLEMS

ECZEMA

Eczema shows itself as itchy, flaky patches of skin which can be red, irritating, and sometimes oozing. Often difficult to cure, it may have a stress, allergy-related, or even hereditary cause. Orthodox treatment usually involves the use of hydrocortisone cream.

As an emergency measure, a cool chamomile Compress can help to relieve itching, and if it is oozing, a drop each of juniper and geranium in a tablespoonful of evening primrose oil can relieve discomfort.

Here is an all-purpose formula:

ECZEMA LOTION

1 drop chamomile
2 drops geranium
2 drops lavender
1 drop sandalwood or benzoin

Dilute in 1 tablespoon of evening primrose oil, or a non-perfumed, light, aqueous cream.

Other useful oils include: Rose otto, neroli, and patchouli.

CELLULITE

Can be caused by hormonal changes in the body and is greatly influenced by circulation, diet, and lifestyle. This problem will not go away without a lot of effort on the part of the sufferer. Book a course of lymphatic drainage massage and be prepared to work hard on yourself. A healthy diet, more exercise, regular skin brushing, and massages are essential.

CELLULITE BLEND

2 drops eucalyptus citriodora
2 drops cypress
1 drop patchouli

Dilute in 2 teaspoons of sweet almond oil.
Brush or loofah your skin before bathing. After bathing, rest for 20 minutes and then apply oil.
Other useful oils include: Grapefruit, lemon rosemary, juniper, and black pepper.

ACNE

Not just an adolescent problem, pimples and blackheads are caused by over-productive sebaceous glands just below the surface of the skin. Refined, sugary and fatty foods should be avoided as much as possible, and the skin kept scrupulously clean. Acne responds well to essential oils, and there are several that can be used as part of a regular routine.

FACIAL OIL/ACNE

1 drop sandalwood
2 drops palmarosa
1 drop lemon
1 drop lavender or chamomile

Dilute in 1 tablespoon of hazelnut or apricot kernel oil. Use night and morning. After first application, apply a warm compress to aid absorption, followed by a second application.

FACIAL SAUNA

1 drop lavender
1 drop juniper or lemon

Blend in a bowl of hot water. Use three or four times a week.

DABBING LOTION

1 drop each tea tree, lemon, lavender oils

Dilute in 2 teaspoons witch hazel.
Use a cotton swab and, with care, dab onto spots.
Other useful oils: Myrtle, neroli, petitgrain, geranium, myrrh.

BROKEN CAPILLARIES

Usually affecting fair and sensitive skins, but also those constantly exposed to sun and wind. Treat with care. Hot baths, saunas, and harsh soaps will not help. Massage the face gently on a regular basis.

FACIAL OIL

1 drop chamomile and/or rose otto

Dilute in 1 teaspoon of macadamia nut or passion flower oil.

CHAPPED HANDS

Often caused by washing hands in cold water and not drying them properly, especially in cold weather.

HAND CREAM/OIL

2 drops benzoin or myrrh
2 drops sandalwood
2 drops lavender

Dilute in 1 tablespoon of macadamia nut oil, or a non-perfumed cream base. Use throughout the day.

SOCIALIZING

SETTING THE SCENE

ATMOSPHERIC BLENDS FOR DIFFUSERS AND FRAGRANCE BURNERS

DINNER PARTY

3 drops petitgrain
2 drops clary sage
2 drops sandalwood
2 drops coriander
or black pepper

MORNING COFFEE

2 drops bergamot
2 drops grapefruit
1 drop myrtle
2 drops juniper

AFTERNOON TEA

3 drops geranium
1 drop rose absolute
3 drops cypress
2 drops sandalwood

FESTIVE SPIRIT

1 drop ginger
3 drops coriander
4 drops orange
2 drops frankincense

PERSONAL PERFUMES

Perfumes are an important part of the social scene – but choosing one is a very individual experience. It's all a matter of preference. Making your own can be great fun, and there is one to suit every occasion. The blends below are intended purely to give you an idea of what is possible – now it's up to you.

Fragrances can be very loosely divided up as follows:

MASCULINE NOTES: Frankincense, sandalwood, vetiver, clary sage, coriander, black pepper, juniper, lemon, grapefruit, jasmine, petitgrain, cypress, or rose otto.

FEMININE NOTES: Benzoin, myrrh, patchouli, ylang ylang, neroli, palmarosa, bergamot, orange, chamomile, lavender, geranium, or rose absolute.

MASCULINE PERFUME

2 drops sandalwood
2 drops frankincense
4 drops petitgrain
4 drops grapefruit
3 drops cypress
2 drops clary sage
1 drop black pepper
1 drop rose otto or jasmine

FEMININE PERFUME

1 drop neroli
2 drops rose absolute
4 drops lavender
4 drops palmarosa
4 drops orange or bergamot
1 or 2 drops patchouli

Dilute in 2 tablespoons of jojoba or coconut oil, or using the method described in the introduction, see page 11.

Whether a blend is masculine or feminine does not, of course, dictate who actually wears it, and many suit either sex. Mix and match, have fun, and remember: the perfumes of nature never stay the same. Constantly changing and moving, every natural scent is a moment of creation – that's what makes it special.

BIBLIOGRAPHY

Davis, Patricia, *Aromatherapy – An A–Z*, C. W. Daniel 1988.
Franchomme, Pierre and Penoel, Dr Daniel, *L'Aromatherapie Exactement*, Jollois 1990.
Grayson, Jane, *The Fragrant Year: Seasonal Meditations with Aromatherapy Oils*, Thorsons/Aquarian 1993.
Ryman, Daniele, *Aromatherapy: An Encyclopedia of Plants and Oils and How They Help You*, Piatkus 1991.
Tisserand, Robert, *The Art of Aromatherapy*, C. W. Daniel 1977.
Wildwood, Chrissie, *Create Your Own Perfumes Using Essential Oils*, Piatkus 1994.

INDEX

Bold page numbers refer to main entries